# A Song About Circles

STEVEN BREYAK

Sagging
Meniscus

Set in Mrs Eaves XL with LaTeX.

ISBN: 978-1-963846-13-3 (paperback)
Library of Congress Control Number: 2024943254

Sagging Meniscus Press
Montclair, New Jersey
saggingmeniscus.com

*For Haruka, who makes it all possible*

# Contents

## I

## II

# III

# IV

# A Song About Circles

I

## Three Dreams of Waking

I.

When I woke in our small boat I knew
only the sound of water. His words were
something else the night had changed.
He had not noticed my sleeping
or chose to ignore it. His story, perhaps,
something he needed to release;
the black world holding him close
and alone for his act. "Every word is true,
I swear," he said, his voice quiet
but everywhere, like an insect's hum.

II.

Before my eyes opened there was the rhythm
of my father's gait. I wasn't sure
where we were going or where I had fallen asleep.
For the moment there was only this.

III.

On the floor in yet another apartment
the building demands my attention.
"I can help you," it says in my dream.
I see me in my room inside of it. "Don't go."
It was a woman, the building, in my dream.
"I just got here," I said aloud, worried and waking.
"Now leave me alone." Then I left and told everyone
how we had slept together.

# Internet Self Search

A close friend in New Jersey whose name I will not disclose
googled herself some years ago and discovered
that she in fact lived in Germany where she taught
at gymnasium and painted breathtaking murals
throughout Munich and Berlin. She emailed
me pictures. "I had no idea of my potential," she wrote
with an lol. "I always knew you had it in you," I teased with a wink.

Having herself just finished art school, and her cardboard canvases
getting no attention in Hoboken, my friend began keeping tabs
on her proceedings overseas. A blog was started and eventually
an entire dot-com was devoted to her anomaly. Within a year
of her self discovery she—the German she—was sited
all over Europe, her work maturing to this new worldliness that stunned
even me, really, almost to tears. Even on a computer screen
her work was so alive. My friend's site grew more sardonic in step,
and hits were coming from all over the Net; she was a comic success.

But on a real-life visit she seemed unstrung. "You should get out,"
I told her. "There's more to you than this." Her eyes darted at me
like a 2 a.m. conspiracy link. "I can't leave now. Have you seen what I've done
to the Zurich billboard show?" It was funny. I couldn't help but laugh
despite my worry. "I'm making it. I can feel it," she said. And like a virus
it was true; within a week she was appearing in New York galleries.

"I'm scared," my friend said. "Don't worry," I told her, "she's not coming
to take your life, that's only in fairy tales." "No, I'm nervous.
What if we burn out too soon?" "My dear, your work is far too good
for that. Did you see what you did to that metro station? I never knew
such things were possible." "That's very sweet of you,
but this is New York. This could make or break me." "Darling,"
I told her, "you're fading, I can't even hear you anymore."

## Popular Program

On the screen there is an actor. The actor
is interacting with non-actors and we catch
it all thanks to carefully placed cameras
and a carefully worded script. We know

there is a script, but we believe it could be
true. We believe someone else could do
and say these things and mean them.

And because the script could be true
the rest of the act becomes real.
Those regular people—or who we're told
are regular people by the narrator—may

or may not be part of the paid act. But just like
the actor, who was once only an informercial
hand up in the audience, they are remade by it.

Where is the thought among us? In the speaker
mouths in every corner of the room,
on every tethered screen the script
runs through. And now our collective mind

reworks the script from what could happen
into hardcoded dreams of what should be.
When the actor returns the enemy is more fierce

and we are more righteous. I used to watch
those old reels of men in conveyor-belted uniforms
shouting malignant programs into their audiences
and wonder: how could this ever happen?

Now I wonder how it continues
ever since, everywhere, and in so many thoughts.
How did the parties route into each of our minds?

## Pleated Pants, Funny Hats, Sometimes Fatigues

When we all wore uniforms our coats
became our clothes. I grew used to being naked
around the others, but in those moments
of coming and going we could be anyone else.

## Federal Bureau of Domestic Drawers

Every time I turn away the details change their place.
Where Stalin cut out comrades like old lovers, our agents
busy themselves blurring home economics: mixing
the enemy's recyclables and cracking refrigerator doors.

Our doubts and fears of us and them have grown so that peering
into my own bureau I find evidence of security. That old watch of mine
has somehow made a move, my photos have been shopped around
to other faces. These worthless treasures blendered, but why?

My sock drawer's headline lining is being rephrased, a Gideon's
man is forever tweaking the family Bible: every edit
so minute the letters move like hour hands. With each remake
my home videos grow more blurry, my life more granulated.

I've lost all faith in reason. The narrative to this story of my stuff
has become so tangled that a child must be behind the curtain, shifting
my gaze only because he can. All that I think will remain
in this adaptation of me is the feeling that I once felt a certain way.

## Human Solutions: Growth Capacity

Everything's gotten smaller.
It's the age of the small.
Tiny men are in my phone
and on my email in their tiny way
paying big attention, ready to send
very large men pouring through my window
to remove me to a tiny undisclosed location.

All of this to build tiny hopes and tiny fears
in all of us: tiny thoughts of winning;
of this being some kind of game; of being
on the right side; of being on the right side and winning.

## On Soft Terror

How many public sinks left running for ghost hands?
Your change given in foreign coins and still
coming up short. Imagine all the salt shakers
loosened upon the world; names scrawled into sidewalks;
people who hate people and work in services
you have to tip; patrons making waitresses cry right now.
Right now there are sleeper cells waiting to hit you
hard on the shoulder as you make your way home.

When I can finger someone who looks responsible
for these acts I follow them home; dump their trash cans;
throw a brick through a window; take a long piss
on the front door. Harsh, yes, but half measures are what
brought us to these times. When those sirens wail for me
I know I am an ancient god, running from all I've done.

# Digestives

"Like a twentieth-century dream of Europe—all horrors, and pastries"
—Laura Kasischke

Into the oven the soldiers push the tarts.
Out they come bubbling with cherries too hot
to touch, though someone always does. The burn
a small price to pay for the sweet red juice
sucked away. The others laugh, take turns.

The surprise when we remember how close
these tastes are: cousins in the mouth. A hungry bite
might draw our own savory blood. Only when
we get older do we keep from sucking the wound.
And only then when we might be caught.

The man with rubber gloves and a baked apple
presses the knife down, pinning the hot bag
of flesh to the board. A puddle forms and the red-gold skin
finally gives. He sighs, looks up with a wink
to his coworker chuckling at the register.

Stealing from candy shops, breaking the glass
to get to the sweets, whether diamond or caramel,
the rush of consuming is a lazy substitute
for taking. The garter snake gorging on mouse pups
must want to groan with pleasure and agony.

The chiffon cake looks so soft that she can't help but squeeze.
At first only a stolen touch to test its buoyancy.
Then two fingers find a fat turn and pinch.
There's a little squeal that escapes as she looks about
for witnesses. And so she must reach down
with her whole palm and rip into this sweet peace.

There were the trenches, gas masks, tanks and fighter planes.
There were croissants, baklava, marzipan, and pound cakes.
Something sweet from the pain, something to carry on.
Desserts as wounds and in place of wounds.

# Life Cycle of a Bullet

Pupa bullets in honey-orange hives
neatly shelved at every Kmart and Walmart.
Oddly not Target
                though odder still
at certain bookstores and flower shops.

Small nests you might find twisted
above a door frame or tucked
beneath a rain gutter.
                  Swarms of bullets
ready to pollinate. Enough to snuff
every blossom of every branch of everything.

From each tiny shell a great nothing may spread
its vacuum wings. Drop a few in a shoebox,
plant some under the carseat and wait.
                      Wait for
the right season to shout these little deaths to life.

They seem so simple for their elegance. But nothing
is simple about the disappeared.
                  The picture frame
made ephemeral web, the scatter of emptiness
seeded in the front door are intricately missing.

An instant hole from flesh, the delicate knot
of all of ones thoughts bitten through. Only the horror
is simple. The horror blankets us and makes us all simple.

## The Gunman

enters the room
as a centaur enters a glade.

Everyone feels the miracle at once.
Adrenal glands tear life open

and each breath now imbibed
turns every moment golden.

No one hears the point-and-click
as the demigod works its transmutations.

People made gazelles leap through open windows.
People made hares burrow beneath desks.

People, as always punished for their awe,
made reeds are blown down in a gust.

Each time is more unbelievable than the last.
Then it's not. Grainy videos are made clear in dreams.

The cacophony of the chorus: divisions
drawn too late between our world and another.

No wonder this draw to worship.
Proof of myth exists in burning

a small mixture of charcoal, sulfur
and the mind. As thoughts shrink away

an old god again breathes and consumes
as we stare into what we cannot see.

## An Overlooked Tribe in Rural Pennsylvania

Walking in the woods behind my childhood home
I came across a tribe of little people. Well,
they were maybe 4-foot-something on average
but definitely small enough to group them in a tribe.
That, and they were wearing strange clothes and pointing
spears at me. They looked native, but one never knows.
Haven't you heard of the New World? I asked,
Manifest Destiny, all that? They looked at one another
and then all back to me as if to say, No. Then one spoke.
In English (I know, surprised me too) he told me that others
had happened by, but never seemed to notice them and their life
along this property line between my parents' and Old Man Weeber's.
They asked if I would keep quiet and leave them be. They'd gotten by
generations on small game, spring water and a few wild berry bushes,
and they just wanted to be alone together right where they were. Of course,
I said. Why should they bother me now, after so long unseen? No problem.
They lowered their spears and disappeared, and I tried to remember
some appropriate bit of folklore to give the event context.
I was happy with my luck, both in seeing them and still being alive.
I walked about the rest of the afternoon smiling at trees and shooting
fingers at birds. But when I got back to the house something about
the whole event really irked me. Maybe it was having a spear
shoved in my face on my own property, or just all the potentials
that come with freeloaders and the homeless. Before it was too late
I phoned Immigration, but it was too late. I'd have to wait till morning.

## Human Solutions: Fresh Water

The bottled-water spring gurgles from a hillside
in a glass jug above its tap.

A bottled-water creek stands like dominoes
meandering through the quiet wood.

A storm of 8-ounce water bottles pummels the valley
and rolls into still streams.

The bottled waterfall roared for a moment
before becoming a bottled-water lake.

Ships screech through the calm
of bottled-water oceans.

Bottled-water glaciers, extravagantly labeled
with images of their counterpart, break apart and float away like attention.

## Our Lives as Drivers in a Foreign Film for Cars

Before thoughts of plot can whir to full speed
two vehicles screech their authority. A woman,
a girl really, no more than sixteen, screams; giant
insect it is, a Beetle has come to rest on her leg.

Another woman vacates the car like pieces of glass
from a kaleidoscope. The girl has broken
the elegance between them. The woman circles
the screaming girl-car hybrid and cries to the people

coming out of still more vehicles. She says, "I lost control."
Or I think she says that. It's all happening in another country,
and the cars are clearly the major players,
though I find their silence impossible to follow.

Another person from the other car, it seems,
has run a red light and from her car run out of the scene.
The wind on her face might be saying, "My god,
my god." Her stoic car stays behind and still.

Somewhere in the girl's persistent screams
she must have said something like "Get it off!"
because some men in the crowd do just that, rocking
our protagonist to a tilt, sliding her from its touch.

She falls silent just as the fire truck and ambulance come
to say the things that they may say—something like
"It's all under control. Please return to your vehicles."
The day fades as people disappear into cars and drive off.

It's a confusing film, subtitles or no. It's hard to tell
what an internal-combustion mind makes of these acts:
if they see the tragedy in the many ways they kill us
or find farce in our undying love of their interiors.

## Commuted

The chrome-blue chassis the color of newborn stars
spied cooling through the Hubble is wrong-way down
in a median strip as beautifully maintained as a golf course.
Its oily belly exposed, its wheels turned in on itself.
The ambulance drives away slowly ahead of us in waiting traffic
and into another world.
                    In another pose this car could be in a commercial
instead of the coming night's news: some of us watching and wanting;
some of us lost in the busy morning to come; some of us kissing
some of our necks and dreaming of a life far from this, someday in the stars.

## Hope

High above our dying city a man
soars into the pale blue blanket
that's killing us because we make it
beautiful. His fist mid-slug against
whatever god might be laughing at us.
On comic-book cue the men
in this crowd reach up and crush
the hats they imagine should be there.
As if a fedora or baseball cap would
be the first thing missed if the rules
had suddenly changed.

Physics prevails with her familiar arc. Still
we hope against everything we've ever known;
already this con has won our hearts. We watch
not expecting the impossible upswing, straight up,
up into the sky. We're too tired for prayer,
but it's a kind of faith that makes our eyes follow
his descent. I know I'm not the only one
turning away after it's too late.

## Human Solutions: World Hunger

It's okay. The world will soon be safe
from our drills. What few morsels
remain are, not impossible,
but embarrassing to reach for.
The next course is under way:
Sun and wind. Our appetites
renewed, these words salivate
even the most sparing of us. It will be
a delicious time, covering each green,
undeveloped inch with panels and mills.

## Why This Love Poem Will Never Get Published

You're an interruption. Like the commercials
they show during the Super Bowl, you're the only part
I want to see. You're the crowd overtaking the stage,
dancing to the music that can no longer be played.
You're the fine print, the legalese I can't quite fathom
that somehow puts my life in your balance.

Do you ever wake up with the feeling that something
incredibly important has happened or is still happening
somewhere out of your understanding? You're ancient wars
ending between tribes in the deepest Amazon; you're political prisoners
being freed on planets in the even further outskirts of the Milky Way:
huge events in tiny places so removed from what should be happening,
from what should matter, that no one will ever read about you.

# II

## Touch Memory

The other night while making marinara I cut out a bite-sized
wedge of my fingertip. In a blink the tomato-can lid
jumped unstuck and froze again in me. I stanched
the cut with a paper towel and paced the kitchen, praying
I might avoid the hospital. I bled for hours, but not gushing.
The dime-sized flap of flesh stayed put if I was careful.

Four days later and my wife laughs, "You stare at it too much."
Amazing, my body quietly sealing and fixing me. I can feel there,
a little, mostly pain. Hues of blood are fading and the edge
is smoothing over. My wife still cringes. Blood makes her faint.
Our two-year-old, though scared at first, now begs to touch it.
"Be gentle," I say, "it can still bleed." He says it's a little slice of grapefruit.

Six years ago I left a marriage that from its start was an accident
of avoidances. She and I were more afraid of being alone than growing
to hate one another for not being what we needed. Our love became
our hate and we nursed it. By the end the only thing we felt
for each other was pain. The only way we knew we were there
was to hurt one another. We'd cry, embrace, heal to do it again.

Two a.m. one winter night, drunk and walking alone to that cold home
I crossed a bridge and stopped for a moment and considered jumping
into the black river below. Just a breath or two this thought lasted,
but it was not some whim or invasion. It was promising and terrifying.
The next day I started looking at apartments. For some reason
she begged me to stay. For some reason it hurt so much more to go.

Now I look back at that me and wonder, Who was that? We're lucky
our former selves can't answer for the crimes we remember.
What they might say would be worse than the memories.
Those moments you're standing there, waiting in some line or another
and your mind wanders into a you who didn't even know
he was a monster. Inside we're always bleeding.

Soon I will feel my son's touch again. My wife will find something else
about me that makes her laugh. The pain I caused will fade.
Maybe a scar will still mark my haste, some dead part
that can't be touched. A thin crease might be all that shows
of the wound still there, unnoticed unless I touch it just—
Then it whispers a sudden chill, telling me to care.

## January 22nd, 2020

A summer night three years ago
I met a date for pizza.

A week after we met, I flew to the US
for a month. When I came back
we went out for takoyaki.

I was careful with my heart then.
I think we both were. We had both
mismarried before and were having
another go at youth.

And now she's asleep in the other room
with our son in her arms.

How did something so fragile
left to its own fate
grow into so much of why
I do anything?

Every day brings a happiness
I'd never known before.

## Netflix and Chill

We used to know the best restaurants
and everybody in them. We knew every party
and everyone knew our names. Now we sit and watch
the newborn as if his crib were a TV
we can reach into and feel the warm pressure
of new stories grabbing hold. And just that
is so much bigger than anything until now. That me
before this is someone I know, I remember, but not me.

I expected to grow into this role. Instead a moment
ticked by and the software had changed. Every thought
is now a father's thought. And this is just a tease
to what it must have been for you. Thread by thread
building in you, tearing through you while all
I could do was wait, absorbed in all I couldn't do.
And now this little creature plugs into
you, feeds from you. Our lives' spin-off.

Months later, while I video his first bites
of mashed banana as you hold him in your arms
you'll cry for this beginning, this end. When I ask,
looking through my screen, if you're crying, I'll hear
that I'm crying. We'll laugh and cry. We'll joke
about all the beer and coffee you'll be drinking soon.
We'll celebrate the life growing from us,
over us as we try to take it all in.

## Sleep Training

It feels like teaching you to paint
by breaking all your brushes.
I want to hold you, quiet you,
but it's only made it harder.
How did your mastery of sleep devolve?
You would spend so long in your sleep,
so deeply that we grew scared. 13-hour stretches,
occasionally changing your diaper as you slept on.
It was like we were living a fairy tale. Then it stopped
and you woke up more and more in the night.
The doctor said it was because you had started eating,
you longed for that time when your mother provided
all you needed. So, in time she and I get through these nights,
knowing you don't understand why we are taking this
from you. Now you wake just to be held, and just
saying that hurts my heart. I would carry you
all night, but we all must sleep. When you wake up
and cry to me, raise your hands for me to lift you, then scream
when I just pat you where you lay, it hurts me in a way I hope
you'll never know until you have your own children because
as much as it hurts to help you by denying you, this pain is love.

## Sowing

Early in spring I prepare the window boxes.
Dig out the dead roots, turn the dirt over.
I have no idea if this is what should be done.
I suppose I should search some advice.

I see my two-year-old son through the glass door
and open it, letting in the rushing sound of the city.
"These are seeds," I say, shaking a few into my hand.
I show him where to press them into the dirt.

"These will be basil, and these will be cilantro."
"Basil and Cilantro!" he bursts as if I just made up
these strange names for our project.

We watch over days as the dark earth slowly opens
to the green pushing through and these sprouts
begin to grow up and into this world. "Basil and Cilantro!"

Then something goes wrong. Some weeks in the cilantro
begins to fade. First one plant then all of them whither.
Soon after, the basil, too, fades and dies. All but one.

What can I do? I turn the dirt over and start again
in the cilantro box, pull the dead sprouts out of the basil.
I push down the seeds and hope, to have some life
before he notices, but none of them take.

I know of at least three girls I dated that had abortions
while we were together. I say "girls" because I was just a boy.
Even when I was nearing thirty, I see now that I was just a boy.
To put ourselves in such a place with a shrug . . .
I wish indifference could be a kind of innocence.

Only once did I know before it had happened: the last time.
In another city I sat with K— in a clinic under these high windows.
The weather was beautiful. The oblivious sun shined down on us.
The clinic was so large and crowded it felt like an airport or even a church.

And like an airport or a church, it was all about waiting.
I see now that this was part of it, making us wait.
How many leave? How many grow determined?

We sat there, K— and I, still in love, I think, holding hands.
Not far from us were these two girls. Really girls. Teens.
And like all teens they were in their own world,
unaware that the world we shared encompassed it.

They talked about partying and fucking and how fun
their lives were. They laughed at everything the other said
and then laughed at what they themselves had said.

I remember only one story clearly. The blonde girl
was talking about a boy she fucked at one party
and then later saw at another party where she said hi
and he said, "Do I know you?" and she explained
and he said, "Nah, that wasn't me." "What was that?"
she asked her friend through laughter that I remember fading
into a short silence before they both recovered. I was relieved
by how different I felt we were from them.

All us kids there, playing at making life. (How hard is it,
really, to put on a condom? Yes, every time.) No one to stop us,
no one to say that there might come a future where
a person inhabiting our bodies, with our memories,
will look back at this day for answers, for reasons,
for simply the fact that this day happened.

The next thing I remember is K— and me waiting for the train
when she doubled over then squatted, her head down.
Was she crying? Should I call an ambulance? Before I could
speak, she was standing again. "It's okay," she said, "It happens."

I wonder if it haunts K— and the others I used to play with,
or those two girls at the clinic, or all the others sitting beneath
those high windows that day we were there and all the days we weren't.
If it doesn't, if they have let that moment go, then what have we done
to them? "We" being those who never told them a story like this.

In the end, we had one basil plant. My son was thrilled that anything
was growing. He couldn't see all the life that wasn't there.

## Meeting my Daughter

Your parents, family, childhood friends, girlfriends.
How many people in your life really shape who you become?
Roommates, lovers, neighbors, the rare friendships that have lasted,
the rare friendships found as an adult. Of course spouses, for good and bad,
always more of one than the other. And finally your children.

All these people you meet who help build you or break you
into who you are, they come at you strangers. Not only what
they do, but that they will shape you in anyway. That you will laugh
and cry with and over them, is a mystery, even if you expect it.
Even my first child, as much as I knew I would love him
I didn't know just what I would feel until he was here.

And now my wife and I are awaiting our second child, a daughter.
And for the first time in my life I know I'm about to meet one
of the most important people in my life. I know that for the rest of my life
this person will be in my thoughts before I've even seen her.

## A Toy Story

Attached to the living room in the first place I called home
was a playroom where I could be found between meals
while my mother did things around the house. Robots,
cars, robots my dad could turn into cars, he-men
gnashing their teeth would come alive in a world
that existed between my right and left hands.

I would disappear into that space for hours. My dad
would come home, lower himself to the floor. He'd smile,
"Who's this then? Is he a good one?" I'd answer,
but my eyes stayed fixed on that hermetic world that flew
through the room at the end of my outstretched arms.
Nothing else to do, he'd take up a toy and join in

as I do now with my son. All this time all I want
is for him to look at me. It's not that he doesn't. Only
that every glance is like a beautiful world opening,
I come alive. We're playing with this chair that sings
about shapes in Japanese and English. He's enraptured.
I sit here drained, flagging but working to stay with him.

Then a song about circles
begins to play and my boy
walks into my arms and takes
me in his. He stands here
for a few seconds, a long time
in his world, holding me as I hold him.
My dad died two months ago. I wasn't there. I live
on the other side of the world now. But near the end
I would call most nights—mornings for him—and we could talk
for a time before the phones we held opened another distance.

Anything outside of that world in front of him was a blur.
"How's your breakfast then? Any good?" When I ran out
of sense for him he'd say, "Well . . ." and I'd say, "Okay. Talk
to you tomorrow." And that was it. Day after day until it wasn't.

Just a few minutes
over a few weeks,
but it's all still happening
in my world.

# III

## Ludwig's Sleight of Hand

When I was five my Uncle Ludwig would
pull his thumb off his hand and put it back.
Within two shows I got to know his trick
was in the clumsy way his hand had held

itself, a lack of grace to be the soul
of his show when a buzz saw stole his thumb
over stray thoughts and a knot. The clean trim
through clay skin worked from this hack bit a spell.

In awe I saw that headless nub and thought
he had reached the pinnacle of his act,
studied with Austrian masters secret
hand gestures to make his knuckle forfeit

its tip to enchantment. It must have been
stashed in a drawer or slipped behind my ear
where it waited for his signal to reappear:
an impossible snap of the fingers when
his young audience had all but lost hope.

## Aunt Sophie's Stroke and Me a Child

Though her eyes had kept like marbles,
her tongue was a broken See 'n Say:
people and places but never a story;
her voice a game of Memory.

She was one of those plastic eggs
that tumble from gumball machines,
her mind a kind of candy that quarters can unwind:
so much chalk to so much sugar;
a taste familiar too soon.

## Telephone Sales of Adjustable Beds

She tells me she suffers from everything I read to her.
I tell her that these beds will comfort her, that they're made
for her. She tells me she can't meet the bed man

because she has chemo appointments all week,
and I tell her we can arrange a time, any time to show
her the benefits of the bed, to let the real sleaze,
the real salesman—not me—into her home
so he can work her over like so many cells in her body.

She tells me she has IVs, that she has tubes they, those cold
saviors they, put in and take out. She tells me she has no time.
I tell her good luck with her visits, let her go, and look into my palms.

I'm just too far away to know what I'm looking for:
too deep in no real job, ring tones, and failure; doing things
for money that aren't illegal but certainly criminal. I turn my hands,
spray my fingers across the keyboard, and dial another number.

## Intended Purchase

That summer I would see my mother everywhere.
Any blonde-white bob would give me pause.
Always while shopping, sometimes hours from home.
I was so sure it was her I'd nearly call out.

In the eye is a mirror where the past drifts
over the now. Inside there's a child in a maze
of trees and cliff faces made of clothes
and cereal boxes where I trail behind her.

I was home, visiting and eager to escape.
Time and purchases have always crowded the place.
Every toaster, every canned up pain we'd ever had
is in that house, patiently adding to their ranks.

So I'd see friends, run away to a cafe, stay with cousins.
A moment away was already too much, so why not days?
That's when I'd see her in every middle-aged consumer
and want to hear how her day had led her to this store.

What product could only be found at this outlet mall
halfway to Erie? How is it you found this food court
in Ohio where I've been staring into the orange glow
of a heat lamp over foil-wrapped memories?

Once it actually was her. I was rushing down
grocery-store aisles when I noticed how much
more I needed. My arms full of items falling
from me. She was there. She gave me her cart.

## Helping my Father Fix the Tractor

Eventually I just stood there some feet
from you and watched. It was clear from go
that neither of us was up for this work. Still,
you wouldn't let me leave. After some rifling
around the decaying junk in the dim barn, all that felt left
to do was watch you mutter and then yell at the tractor

you couldn't get to start. I was sure this was punishment,
but I didn't understand why I was receiving it.
You slammed the wrenches that wouldn't do the job back
into the toolbox. I imagined if the engine would just turn
I could escape back to the sofa and old reruns on TV.

But that tractor was old even when you were young.
Bug-eye headlights, that horse-skull engine
like those gangster cars in the funnies
you used to read to me. When I heard mom
pulling the car up the drive, I turned and ran to her.
If I could get to the car and fill my hands
with shopping bags, I could somehow get out
of this work of failing to help in your failure.

I tried to ignore your calls but finally stopped
and turned to you. You said, "You'd rather be
with your mother?" Of course I did. With her
I could be alone. You said something more
that I took for permission and ran off.
Even then, I think, I knew how this hurt.
This strange machine that had broken and would
remain so. I knew I should have come back.

I remember when it did work. Me small enough
to fit in the seat with you, and you letting me steer us
on a wavering, rumbling path through the high grass. I try
to keep this memory going. Though these tools confound me, too.

# Decay Products

A thick Pennsylvania August. I was seven,
picking strawberries with my mom and dad when
three drunks pulled in and idled a car on our front yard.

One stepped out and began pissing on the mailbox.
When my dad yelled, "What the hell," the guy shook
his balls and said, "Why don't you come down
and I'll show you." "I'll be right down," he called
from the porch as he led my mom and me inside.
Dad held the forty-four behind his back as he walked

down the driveway. The drunk again danced
his dick in the burning air, laughing until the gun barrel
hit the side of his head. He fell back into the car,

pants loose, a whimper escaping him. As they sped away
my dad fired three shots into their wake. Unscathed,
they drove through me shattering only an idea

of order into an idea of discord. An example:
I know I should hate my father—risking death,
prison, us over pride—but some

something in me wants to be him for that moment: to hold
that gun to some fool and his mistake; to shed love
in defense of love; to be right

the way certain elements can exist in perfect situations
for only pieces of a second.

# IV

## Stepping from the Cabin

Subway to the airport. Osaka to Pittsburgh. Rent-a-car
nightmare. Pittsburgh to Frazer Township. Predawn. 13-hour
jet lag like amphetamines clicked me on hours ago.
Time passed listening to the wood beams and tin roof creak,
playing at what creature's traversing the woods just outside,
studying the nuances of sleep between my wife
and baby boy. At the first hint of light I make coffee
and head for the porch to watch the sunrise.

Stepping through the door a jolt shakes me. A spider
hangs before my nose. I had forgotten how prevalent
spiders are here. How I used to admire webs
pregnant with morning dew. In Osaka there is no dew,
and I only see spiderwebs occasionally packed thick
along bridge ledges. Country spider, city spider.
My wife would have me kill this one, but she's asleep
so I reach high and catch the thread on my finger.

A jolt again when the spider makes a quick climb
for my hand. I shake the silk away like it's burning,
search for a bite I'm certain I feel, but there's nothing.
I look back and she, the spider, still hangs there. What of what
happened happened? This time I catch the thread.
This time she doesn't move. Maybe she feels
her line arcing and gives way to the breeze I make.
I leave her dangling from the porch where I see other webs

nested in the corners. A good place, I think. Her meals
keeping pests from me and future guests. I feel pretty good
about myself, like I did this spider right. Then I begin
to think about whatever it was that moved me
from my birthplace not far from this cabin to Asia,
to a life better than any I could have dreamed up here:
my wife, our son, a life that affords me this trip
home, time to sit and think up strange thoughts like this.

What finger from the sky moved my mind to fly out there?
Or here, on this page trying to shape the everyday
into something profound, to think someone would ever
care to see through me? I'd like to say to what-if-any hand
responsible, "Thank you" and "I'm terrified wondering where
your will ends and mine begins." I put
the pencil down. The sunrise long past, I look
for the spider and her work, but she's gone.

## The Only Thing Left Is the Ice Cream

The Luddites didn't despise technology so much
as its use. Not their craft being done by machine,
but what the machine made of them.

I don't know which is wrong:
what's passed or what's coming,
the knotted hands or the humming engine.

The same idea of a cloth that once touched
would move some nob to dream of its making, is now
ripped open to sop up soda in a fast-food kitchen.

Beauty is skinned to get to her tools.
But what has beauty in her prime
given us? Callouses, arthritis, eyesight

good for threading a needle but little else.
Where there is art there is suffering. The less
beauty in the world, the more freedom

to appreciate it. I can already search masterworks
from my phone if I'm ever done playing with it.
You see, it's not the fabric but the idea, the mind

that is outmoded, outsourced to the screen.
Giant machines in dimensions of information
don't just do the hard math but thread through

those quiet moments notifications of fun
fun fun. And now everything seems to just seem.
The end of boredom is the end of dreams.

## Caveat Ethos

I want to hold a duck a live duck
in the palm of one of my hands
either hand is okay though I prefer
the left and I don't want it to be forced
or tame or drugged or especially dead
I want a wild duck to rest its balsa-wood body
(no decoys please) in my left palm
of its own freewill if such an animal
can possess freewill otherwise by chance
of course we can take measures
to limit chance but nothing dealing with the duck
or the natural unspoiled setting in which this event
will take place and do not tell me
what these measures will be I don't want to know
I don't even want to know when it will happen
(though I expect soon) I simply want to find myself
unexpectedly in whatever wilderness
(Alaska or something like that) with this duck
(a Mandarin) in my bare left hand. How much?

## Pornography for the Blind

Wake at dawn and before showering run your fingers
through the grass of your front lawn. Invite a friend's spouse
to rearrange your kitchen: grape juice for milk, apple
for onion. Sniff and lick but never ask names. Go hiking
(alone, in spring) find a small clearing then strip and leave
with your hands outstretched into the pines. At gift shops
breathe heavily through wind chimes. In supermarkets
squeeze all produce, delve your hands into boxes of grain,
coerce cashiers to reach into the fold of your wallet
and count out what you owe. Trust their change. Late at night
climb gracelessly into a mysterious neighbor's pool.
Change strokes often: freestyle then butterfly, breast then back.

## Before Photo
## (From a Weight-Loss Ad)

The past is nothing but wrong. There's the fifty pounds
but the electric hasn't been paid either. The expensive flashlight
her dull husband bought on credit at the Kmart cannot be found
in the junk drawers or cardboard boxes or floors of closets.
There is a camera though, a disposable; how wonderful
he should find that. She insists that it's easier to see without it,
but he's oblivious to her still. He holds the camera at arm's length
and takes a few steps between shots. "Let your eyes adjust,"
she pleads. But he's having too much fun, giggling with each click
from too many beers and in spite of missing his sitcoms. The flash peels
across her face. She hears that cricket sound as he winds the film
and can feel it in her stomach. Everything is orange and black and
everywhere she looks there is the chemical purple blotch of a flashbulb.
He laughs, "You should have seen your face."

                                                  And then there is After.
Shoulders back, every light in the house burns again. Her skin
another bulb, a vaseline gleam to her cheeks. Who knows,
who cares where he is. The cameraman here now knows
how to take a picture, how to coerce a smile, that scar that gleams
so white across her face.

## Heart Crane

Surgeons prep the heart crane and cameras.
Fibers float down like angelic sea limbs until they strike
at the chest. Titanium pulleys whir as the heart is lifted
then gently lowered. All in the operating theatre hush.

High above a skyscraper, hidden away from most,
a raw ticker drips through a bucket's teeth. The heart crane
operator takes a candy bar from his lunchpail, a fiery swig
from his thermos. Hard-hatted men clear him an opening.

The fishbone ribs of the ship hold fast on the choppy water.
And yet the heart crane breaks. Passengers and crew
know not what to do.

The heart crane on straw-thin legs tiptoes the shallows,
searching past mollusk and seaweed
for the remnant of some dire act.

## One-Fingered Man Fails in Everest Bid
## (from an RSS Feed)

Who wakes up knowing what news they'll become by afternoon?
Some, I'm sure, strive for the odd combination
to capture the world's fascination if only for the time
to click to link and blink a moment in wonder. But imagine

the plain, turning days rolling this man forward without knowledge
of the music drafted in his tracks. One day buying airfare
on a touchscreen. Another day folding clothes. Then one afternoon
he's approaching the stratosphere, feeling drunk and alone,

remembering clearly each finger's small but tremendous
death as if they happened in someone else's hands
but had been transposed to his by the same cruel magic
that led him to love this mountain, to come apart in its cold stomach.

The music keeps rolling his bid to its surreal crescendo, raising
his one digit again and again. Always there on the mountain,
yet, in light blotches behind his eyes and in his air-starved
mind, for fractions of moments passed the idea of "bid"

places him in an auction house. All around him—the walls,
the chairs, the people—exists in a flash of luxury. All except
for him. Wounded and in his gear and filth he outbids the few
who still care to purchase this dead craft, this climbing of Everest.

Bidding with nothing but breath in a life where this climb is nothing
until a man who seemed so like us loses everything for his art.
And then only for a blip between all this pressing
through screens do we wonder at what he remembered.

## Distilled Life with Mixed Reviews

Wrapped in a gauze shroud of mystery
sequined in misplaced puzzle pieces,
our virtuoso's soul can only be revealed
in future thick books and this here poem

about his latest works: the installations
that don't look installed, the paintings
made paintings by a frame. O his marriages,
his lovers, his disappointing children! It's all there

in the drip drop and crinkle, the squiggle
and the splat. And how those pedigree critics scoff,
call his work re-hatched abstract. What good
is genius when doubt is as real and vague

as that orgasm creation? Too often
his only solace is in his mite's progression
along his section of this strange creature,
the arts. He giggles, chews a cuticle

as he studies his pallet or litters a room.
The world contains so many mistaken
mistakes. But for a short time, in a small place,
he can make the necessary corrections.

## What I Learned in Bill Knott's Poetry Workshop

A wild horse
is a beautiful thing.
The decision
to break (an unpleasant
though accurate term)
is difficult. One
must not urge
the talent that may emerge.
The most powerful
and most determined
can be as poor a choice
as the most graceful.
Even those with promise
can buck or founder
after showing steady composure.
Still, some spend their hearts
training instinct
to precision, flight
into a craft. And it was through
the strangest of luck
that my breaking course
was taught by a feral horse.

## The Matter with Me at Poetry Readings

The reader and I, our eyes meet
for a moment by chance, and when they do I know
she hates me a little for being here. Everyone else
in this section of the bookstore stares and smiles
like twenty or so proud parents. And here I am,
as uncomfortable in my folding chair
as in my Goodwill blazer, my leg jumping
at ten times her rhythm, my gaze swimming over
everything but her. Like a lover so enthralled
he never closes his eyes or makes a sound, I ignore
my responsibility to what's happening here.
Instead of giving a quiet nod as I hold my chin,
I leave her for her words, follow her voice
to that uppermost corner
of the last bookshelf,
where cobwebs grow
as unnoticed as literature.
I see her poem there
the way I might see
the rustling of a deer
in late-autumn, bolting
up a tree-thick hillside
towards some final refuge.

※

# Acknowledgments

Poems in this collection have appeared in the following publications:

- — 3:AM Magazine: *Decay Products, Ludwig's Sleight of Hand*
- — 42Opus: *Three Dreams of Waking; Aunt Sophie's Stroke and Me a Child; On Soft Terror*
- — Exacting Clam: *A Toy Story; Touch Memory; January 22nd, 2020; Stepping from the Cabin*
- — Existere: *The Matter with Me at Poetry Readings*
- — Gargoyle: *The Gunman; What I Learned in Bill Knott's Poetry Workshop; Helping My Father Fix the Tractor*
- — Live Nude Poems: *One-Fingered Man Fails in Everest Bid; Netflix and Chill*
- — Night Train: *Before Photo, Internet Self Search*
- — Poets and Artists: O&S: *Why This Love Poem Will Never Be Published*
- — Sawbuck: *Pleated Pants, Funny Hats, Sometimes Fatigues*
- — Softblow: *Caveat Ethos (as "Late-Stage Freedom: Caveat Ethos"); Human Solutions: Growth Capacity (as "Newthink: Small")*
- — Thieves Jargon: *Pornography for the Blind; Our Lives as Drivers in a Foreign Film for Cars*
- — Word Riot: *Telephone Sales of Adjustable Beds*

Further thanks to Bill Knott, Aaron Anstett, John Repp, Kathleen Rooney, James Hoffman and all the others who made these poems possible through our discussions and their encouragement. A special thanks to Mark Halliday: reading Tasker Street made me want to be poet and through that sent me stumbling around the world.

After finishing a graduate degree, Steven Breyak left Boston for what was supposed to be a year abroad. After seventeen years in Osaka, Japan he returned to the US with a wife and two children. This collection, in part, tries to capture this chance transition.

www.ingramcontent.com/pod-product-compliance
Lightning Source LLC
Chambersburg PA
CBHW020218090426
42734CB00008B/1125